Philosophy for children

From child to children

Once upon a time!

Not everything should be listened to!

Coloring story!

By: Bernardo Octaviano Pereira

This book
belongs to:

I dedicate this work, firstly, to my parents who I love so much, to my teachers, to my dear aunts and to all my friends, may God bless you all infinitely!

Bernardo Octaviano Pereira

13/04/2024

Once upon a time, in a place, not far from here, several mice wanted to taste a special cheese, which for the mice was the most delicious in the region, however, to reach the much-desired cheese,

they would
have to climb
all the floors
of the building,
which had a
restaurant
where the
cheese was.

The journey began with enthusiasm, but soon on the first floor one of the mice murmured - It's too high, I won't continue;

Other mice, influenced by giving up, will also decide to return and go down too. On the second floor other excuses will arise

- *There are many steps to climb, I give up, I won't continue, and other mice also gave up on climbing, and on the third floor another mouse spoke;*

- *I'm tired, I'm going back, some more mice came back too, and on the fourth floor another mouse spoke;*

- This cheese isn't that tasty, it's not worth that much effort;
And other mice will give up too.

The sequence was repeated on the next floors, with people giving up due to tiredness and lack of motivation.

Only one brave little mouse persevered until he reached the top floor, where he enjoyed eating so much delicious cheese.

When going back down, the other mice, curious and impressed, wanted to know what the secret was of so much determination, of not having given up on climbing so many steps;

He was deaf, so he couldn't hear what the other mice were talking about, the voices that tried to discourage him.

This taught others that we should not listen to negative words, which can make us give up on our dreams and goals.

The end!